Still Small Voice

A 365 Day Devotional Volume 1

Winter

Jean Ann DiBenedetto

WESTBOW
PRESS®
A DIVISION OF THOMAS NELSON
& ZONDERVAN

WestBow Press books may be ordered through booksellers or by contacting:

WestBow Press
A Division of Thomas Nelson & Zondervan
1663 Liberty Drive
Bloomington, IN 47403
www.westbowpress.com
844-714-3454

Cover Illustration by Nick DePasquale
http://njdepasquale.com

ISBN: 978-1-6642-3214-3 (sc)
ISBN: 978-1-6642-3213-6 (e)

Library of Congress Control Number: 2021908198

Print information available on the last page.

WestBow Press rev. date: 05/17/2021

Endorsements

❖ *I have known Jean Ann and her family for over thirty years. Her passion for ministering to people has been an outstanding means of reaching people and presenting to them the saving knowledge of her Savior Jesus Christ. As a published author I was honored to preview her manuscript. She is a shining light in a dark world. Her life stories are inspirational and anointed. I'm looking forward to receiving a copy of her book so I can pass it on to the hurting and struggling in this present world.*
Rev. Daniel R. Schafer - Founder and President Crisis Intervention International LLC, United States Secret Service

❖ *Jean Ann is a firebrand for serving God! Reading her words is like hearing her voice. Through her pen readers can hear her heart of passion for the Lord. Daily connection with the Lord is her goal and sharing her encounters is the goal of this book.*
Rev. Carl Colletti, Former Superintendent for the NJ District of the Assemblies of God.

❖ *Every Christian should possess a copy of this daily devotional. You will hear the Still Small Voice of the Holy Spirit speak to you as you read it and apply it to your daily life. This devotional will speak to your soul; it will encourage you; and it will lift your faith to a new level. A must read for everyone!*
Rev. Richard Martinez, D.Min.,Dean & Director, NJ School of Ministry, Pastor, Community Gospel Church, Northvale, NJ.

❖ *I have known Jean Ann for over thirty years. She has always been a person committed to the Word of God, to the presence of God, to seeing people come to the saving knowledge of Jesus Christ, and to experience the transforming power of God. Jean Ann is someone who has the great ability to speak truth from the heart relating it to your heart and life. This devotional is no different, it will speak to your heart because it is spoken from the heart. It is personal, applicable, practical and inspirational, but is also filled with emotion, which is Jean Ann, but it will challenge you spiritually. Anyone reading through this devotion will find themselves growing personally and spiritually.*

Dr. James W. Wickham, Church Planter &
Pastor, Living Word Community Church

❖ *When you want to describe a person that is dedicated, passionate, energetic, a little crazy....then look no further. From the first time I met Jean Ann jokes followed by laughter followed by deep theological expressions of how the word has impacted her life was a common occurrence. When I heard her testimony I knew that God had given Jean Ann a creative miracle as he gave her the tools she needed to carry out his will. Jean Ann traveled with me on many missions trips to various countries preaching, singing, playing her musical instrument and showing love to those less fortunate then herself. To sum up Jean Ann she has a heart of gold and her whole life has been wrapped around the gospel.*

Michele Lyn McKenna, Former Women's Director
of the New Jersey Ministry Network

Introduction

Started on Wednesday February 6, 2008 – completed September 2019. I had to take my own pill as busyness of life, responsibilities and the many hats of a *Wife, Mother, Mother-in- law, Aunt, Sister, Niece, Sister-in-law, Friend, Church Member, Minister,* and *Nonna* and listen to my Heavenly Father's **Still Small Voice**. I realize the list is unending and for that reason this book was written.

Hats of life…

Nurse	Comforter
Doctor	Coach
Cook	Prayer warrior
Maid	Seamstress
Taxi driver	Interior decorator
Tutor	Meal planner
Referee	Event planner
Guidance counselor	Bookkeeper
Provider	Secretary
Banker	Shopper

In all actuality the list is unending and for that reason it's all too easy to be consumed, resulting in the last thing on our mind which is to listen to our Heavenly Father's **Still Small Voice**. Be that as it may, there is no better way to put it other than a line in the old song; What a Friend We Have in Jesus.

> Oh, what peace we often forfeit
> Oh, what needless pain we bear
> All because we do not carry
> Everything to God in prayer[11]

---

[1] *What A Friend We Have In Jesus*, Words by Joseph Scriven, Music by Charles C. Converse, 1866, Public Domain.

The purpose of this book is to start your busy day with a nugget of encouragement and a reminder to not make a single move until you hear YOUR Heavenly Father's *Still Small Voice*.

Remember what He says in His Word...

> *For I know the thoughts that I think toward you, says*
> *the Lord, thoughts of peace and not of evil, to give you*
> *a future and a hope. (Jeremiah 29:11)(NKJV)*

Why not trust The One who knows your future? Is there anyone else that you know who knows your future? Exactly...so the only way to avoid having a bad day is to listen to His *Still Small Voice*.

Dedication

I want to dedicate this devotional to my beautiful gifts from God...my grandchildren, Nina, Anna, Salvatore, Zachary, Caleb and Gideon. I want them to know that their Nonna loves Jesus with all her heart and wants them to serve Him forever. I know they, as we all, will need new strength every day to serve Him. In knowing that, I want to give this book as a tool to help start their day off right. I love you Nina, Anna, Salvatore, Zachary, Caleb and Gideon...you are the loves of my life. God has blessed me with you! I love you so very much and my biggest prayer for you is that you NEVER walk away from Jesus. KNOW that HE LOVES YOU! Please... always keep Jesus #1 in your life, don't do ANYTHING until you hear His *still small voice*. I love you!!! *Nonna*

Dear God,

   Please Father, anoint my hands as I venture to put on paper what I am hoping will encourage, strengthen, challenge and change those who pick it up day after day and that it will be just what's needed. Please let these pages bring glory and honor to You as each one is an excerpt of messages that I believe You have given me to bring to Your people throughout the past years.

Your daughter who loves You so very much,
Jean Ann

First of all, I want to thank some very good friends of mine, Joe & Sue McKeon who opened their cabin in the Poconos to me so that I could have some time to be alone and seek the Lord. I am in such a cabin where the pot belly stove is blaring, their Bose radio glorifying God with instrumental worship softly ushering me into the Presence of God. The décor is rustic with black bear accents. As I look out the windows all I can see are tall trees stretched toward the heavens, while small blankets of snow still linger on the rocky, hilly ground. Oh, don't let me forget that right on the wall beside the pot belly stove is a beautiful plaque which reads: *Be still and know that I am God.*

With that, I'd like to venture to produce a book that will do just that... allow those who pick it up daily to Be still and know that God is God!

Throughout the years I've purchased and some given to me as gifts, numerous daily devotionals. Unfortunately, I always seem to go back to the same one; Streams in the Desert written in 1925 by Mrs. Charles E. Cowman. I cannot even remember the year I first started reading that book. It is so good I've given many away. I believe the Lord spoke to my heart and led me to write one of my own. You see the words written in this book will not be my feelings alone, but *messages that have been birthed through prayer and fasting,* that have been delivered to the hearts of the people. These messages came from my Heavenly Father in times when I needed to hear from Him.

A personal word:
While in prayer the words **Still Small Voice** rang in my heart. I knew it was to be the title for this book. In I Kings 19, Elijah who was a great man of God found himself in a deep depression. The Lord sent an angel to appear to him not once, not twice but three times to encourage him to get up and go forward. Yet Elijah found himself in a cave feeling helpless, hopeless and in despair. This time the Lord Himself spoke to Elijah and told him to go to the mouth of the cave because He wanted to speak to Elijah.

Vs. 11, 12 says that the Lord passed by and a great and a strong wind rent the mountains, and brake in pieces the rocks before the Lord; but the Lord was not in the wind; and after the wind and earthquake; but the Lord was not in the earthquake; and after the earthquake a fire; but the Lord was not in the fire; and after the fire a still small voice. <u>THE LORD WAS IN THE STILL SMALL VOICE.</u> *(I Kings 19:11-12)*(NKJV)

Many times, we are like Elijah, we know God and yet we may be in a situation that we need to hear His voice but nothing is happening. We try and try but hear nothing and before you know it we are so discouraged that we don't even feel the desire to pray any longer. Guilt begins to accuse us of reasons why God is not answering our prayer. We are no different than Elijah; oftentimes we are waiting for the big "sign" from God. We are waiting...and waiting...and waiting...and nothing. Now we feel "dead". Listen, it's not always in the big "sign", many times we are to just listen and like the plaque on the wall says: *Be still and know that I "God" am God.*

With that I pray as you open the pages to this book day after day it will be with an expectancy to hear His ***still small voice.***

January 1

ADDICTED TO THE GOSPEL
OF JESUS CHRIST

Watch, stand fast in the faith, be brave, be strong.
Let all that you do be done with love.
I urge you, brethren—you know the household of Stephanas,
that it is the first fruits of Achaia, and that they have devoted
themselves to the ministry of the saints—that you also submit
to such, and to everyone who works and labors with
(I Corinthians 16:13-16) (NKJV)

Stephanas was a follower of Paul and a believer in the word Paul preached. He helped Paul immensely.

To be addicted is the give oneself up to; (some strong habit)

Stephanas devoted himself to the word that Paul preached which we know was the gospel of Jesus Christ. Shall we say he was addicted to the Gospel of Jesus Christ?

- Know what you believe and why
- Hold strong to your beliefs
- Know why you are doing it and do it in love

God is not looking for performance but for a genuine heart, passion for Him which will result in compassion for others. {Wouldn't it be nice to be addicted to the Word of God?}

January 2

AM I READY?

*But I do not want you to be ignorant, brethren, concerning those who
have fallen asleep, lest you sorrow as others who have no hope.
For if we believe that Jesus died and rose again, even so
God will bring with Him those who sleep in Jesus.
For this we say to you by the word of the Lord, that we who are
alive and remain until the coming of the Lord will by no means
precede those who are asleep. For the Lord Himself will descend
from heaven with a shout, with the voice of an archangel, and with
the trumpet of God. And the dead in Christ will rise first. Then we
who are alive and remain shall be caught up together with them in
the clouds to meet the Lord in the air. And thus, we shall always be
with the Lord. Therefore comfort one another with these words.
(I Thessalonians 4:13-18)(NKJV)*

Paul founded the church in Thessalonica but his ministry was prematurely
terminated because of intense Jewish hostility. Because Paul had to leave
Thessalonica abruptly, his young converts only had minimal instruction
on how to live a Christian life. He sent Timothy back to check up on
them, but the report was disappointing to Paul, so he wrote I & II
Thessalonians,

- To commend those who were holding on to their faith in the
  midst of persecution.
- To instruct on holiness and godly living
- To clarify certain beliefs.

We as believers must be holy and the gospel must be accompanied by the power and manifestation of the Holy Spirit. {Lord, am I holding onto my faith? Am I living a life pleasing to you?}

Remember...the *still small voice*.

January 3

OUR SECURITY BLANKET

He who dwells in the secret place of the Most High
Shall abide under the shadow of the Almighty.
I will say of the LORD, "He is my refuge and my fortress;
My God, in Him I will trust." (Psalm 91:1, 2)(NKJV)

The secret place is our daily communion in God's presence. The most high shows He's greater than (ANY) threat.

The almighty shows He is greater than (ANY) enemy. The Lord shows He is (ALWAYS) with us and MY God expresses the intimacy, closeness.

- Commune daily with Him
- Know He is all powerful!
- He is Lord over all!
- Get close enough to Him so that you can hear His *still small voice.*

January 4

HAPPY BIRTHDAY SARAH!

Sarah
Meaning: Princess

Today is my daughter-in-law Sarah's birthday. She serves alongside my son, her husband, Vincent as he is a lead pastor. Sarah had to overcome much in our family as she was born and raised in the State of Iowa and everyone knows that those in New Jersey are...well...can I say in your face? Ha-ha! Not to mention being grafted into a loud Italian family who likes to eat and yell at the drop of a hat. (Only an Italian would understand that, ha-ha)!

Sarah has given my husband and I three beautiful grandsons and teaches them the ways of the Lord. She likes Hallmark movies and has mastered the art of baking cookies. I want to pray for her today and ask God in faith to bless her, strengthen her and keep her healthy, wealthy and wise. In Jesus Name.

Not always do we agree, but I love her and bless her. Do you know someone today that you don't always agree with? Don't hold a grudge, send a little note of love and appreciation and learn to enjoy life. God bless you Sarah!

January 5

LORD GOD, WHAT DO YOU WANT ME TO DO?

Now the word of the LORD came to Jonah (Jonah 1:1)(NKJV)

Jonah was directed by God to go to Nineveh, but that was not Jonah's desire, so he fled. He boarded a ship going in another direction and while on the ship the Lord sent a great storm. In fear of sinking the shipmates were throwing cargo overboard while Jonah was fast asleep in the bottom of the boat. When they realized the storm was because Jonah was running from God's presence, upon Jonah's request, they cast him into the sea. There he was swallowed up by a whale. After being in the belly for three days and three nights Jonah cried out to the Lord and as usual the Lord had mercy on Jonah.

- It's not always someone else's fault when things are not going right
- Are you asleep in the bottom of the boat?
- Has the Lord spoken to you?

God had mercy on Jonah and He'll have mercy on you too.
You're not sure what God wants you to do? Listen to that ***still small voice.***

January 6

KEEP YOUR FOCUS

A Psalm of David

Bless the Lord, O my soul;
And all that is within me, bless His holy name!
Bless the Lord, O my soul,
And forget not all His benefits:
Who forgives all your iniquities,
Who heals all your diseases,
Who redeems your life from destruction,
Who crowns you with lovingkindness and tender mercies,
Who satisfies your mouth with good things,
So that your youth is renewed like the eagle's.
The Lord executes righteousness
And justice for all who are oppressed.
He made known His ways to Moses,
His acts to the children of Israel.
The Lord is merciful and gracious,
Slow to anger, and abounding in mercy.
He will not always strive with us,
Nor will He keep His anger forever.
He has not dealt with us according to our sins,
Nor punished us according to our iniquities.
For as the heavens are high above the earth,
So great is His mercy toward those who fear Him;
As far as the east is from the west,
So far has He removed our transgressions from us.
As a father pities his children,
So, the Lord pities those who fear Him.

For He knows our frame;
He remembers that we are dust.
As for man, his days are like grass;
As a flower of the field, so he flourishes.
For the wind passes over it, and it is gone,
And its place remembers it no more.
But the mercy of the Lord is from everlasting to everlasting
On those who fear Him,
And His righteousness to children's children,
To such as keep His covenant,
And to those who remember His commandments to do them.
The Lord has established His throne in heaven,
And His kingdom rules over all.
Bless the Lord, you His angels,
Who excel in strength, who do His word,
Heeding the voice of His word.
Bless the Lord, all you His hosts,
You ministers of His, who do His pleasure.
Bless the Lord, all His works,
In all places of His dominion.
Bless the Lord, O my soul! (Psalm 103:1-22)(NKJV)

BENEFITS OF KEEPING YOUR FOCUS
ON THE LORD JESUS CHRIST

- Forgives
- Heals
- Redeems us
- Kind
- Merciful
- Satisfies
- Renews our youth

- Shows righteousness & justice for the oppressed
- Gracious
- Slow to anger
- Removed our sins
- Compassionate

His mercy, forgiveness and compassion are (FOREVER) ON DOWN TO YOUR CHILDREN!

{Why not keep your eyes on Jesus -is there anyone else like Him?}

January 7

JUMP IN-THE WATER'S GREAT!

God is our refuge and strength, A very present help in trouble.
Therefore, we will not fear, Even though the earth be removed,
And though the mountains be carried into the midst of the sea;
Though its waters roar and be troubled, Though the mountains
shake with its swelling. Selah There is a river whose streams
shall make glad the city of God, (Psalm 46:1-4)(NKJV)

Be still, and know that I am God;
I will be exalted among the nations,
I will be exalted in the earth! (Psalm 46:10)(NKJV)

God's river is a continual flow of His grace, glory, and power in the midst of His faithful people. This river flows from God the Father, Son and Holy Ghost. It flows continually form the throne of God to His people.

VS.10 be still in the Hebrew means, "let go"

Quit holding onto things that keep you from God having His place in your life. He is your refuge- (shelter in times of danger) and your strength. (He enables you to overcome obstacles in life.

God is a very present help in time of trouble. Are you facing something too big for you to handle?

Let go.... jump into the river of God and He shall make you glad.

How? Oh Lord, this is so very hard for me right now but help me to trust you. I'm letting go but I need to hear you. Remember...the *still small voice*.

January 8

LIGHT THE FIRE

When the Day of Pentecost had fully come, they were all with one accord in one place. And suddenly there came a sound from heaven, as of a rushing mighty wind, and it filled the whole house where they were sitting. Then there appeared to them divided tongues, as of fire, and one sat upon each of them (Acts 2:1-3)(NKJV)

Fire may symbolize consecrating and separating believers unto God.

We need the fire (empowerment by the Holy Spirit) to live with the necessary wisdom and revelation to live a life of victory. You can try on your own, but it will take the fire of God to burn up the old habits. The fire brings the Word and the anointing together thus creating in us a beautiful fragrance to God.

Seek ALL that God has for you today, {Lord, fill me with Your Holy Spirit}

January 9

FROM DAYS TO MINUTES

In the words of Jesus

I am the true vine, and My Father is the vinedresser. Every branch in Me that does not bear fruit He takes away; and every branch that bears fruit He prunes, that it may bear more fruit. You are already clean because of the word which I have spoken to you. Abide in Me, and I in you. As the branch cannot bear fruit of itself, unless it abides in the vine, neither can you, unless you abide in Me. I am the vine, you are the branches. He who abides in Me, and I in him, bears much fruit; for without Me you can do nothing. (John 15:15)(NKJV)

One of the fruit is longsuffering which means bearing injuries, insults, trouble, etc. patiently for a long time. Another fruit is faithfulness-continued, steadfast adherence to a person or thing to which one is bound by duty or oath.

Years back the church longed for the touch of the Master's hand so greatly that they spent days at a time in church. In the day of Pentecost, they tarried for fifty days. Children of God wore a smile because they knew they had the victory. Today we are too busy to spend days; we may even be too busy to spend minutes seeking God.

- Do you need fruit from the vine? Are you tired, facing difficulties that make you want to run away from it all? Which vine are you connected to?

Jesus died once and for all, you need not cry and fret…He is right here, right now. Cry out to Him; let Him know you want to be connected to the vine. Let Him know you want His fruit to be seen in your life. You still do have the victory!

- Don't rush God...Listen to His *still small voice*.

January 10

WHAT'S YOUR BURNING BUSH?

And the Angel of the LORD appeared to him in a flame of fire from the midst of a bush. So, he looked, and behold, the bush was burning with fire, but the bush was not consumed (Exodus 3:2)(NKJV)

Moses was in the presence of a bush that was burning out of control and yet it was not consumed. How can that be? God wanted to speak to Moses and He did it in a way that really got Moses' undivided attention.

- Are you in a situation that seems to be burning out of control?

DON'T WORRY! Moses heard God speak through the bush but he was looking that way.

- You will hear God's voice when you're looking towards Him. Don't run from your situation. Maybe you didn't cause it but you're in it. If you look towards God, He will speak to you through that very same situation.

And remember: the bush was not consumed.

- Your family will not be consumed either.

What's your burning bush? God may be allowing it to deliver someone. God sees their oppression; you may be the key to get them out.

- Listen to the voice of God in the midst of the burning bush.

Whatever He tells you to do, He will be with you.

January 11

PASSOVER – FEAST OF UNLEAVENED BREAD

It's the first of three great festivals honored by the Israelite people. It's a celebration of when the Israelites were slaves in Egypt and were directed to put blood of a lamb on all doorposts as a signal to God that He should "pass over" their houses when the death angel passes by.

Feast of Unleavened Bread (celebrated on the fourteenth day of the first month)

Unleavened bread was used in this celebration to show that the people had no time to put leaven in their bread as they ate their final meal as slaves in Egypt. (Leaven is yeast)

Till this day Jewish people all over the world still celebrate this time remembering what their Lord has done.

- Do you remember what the Lord has done in your life?
- Do you celebrate the day of your freedom?
- Oh, how He loves you…. every day with Jesus is a day of celebration for it is a day of freedom!

January 12

VICTORY IN JESUS

But He was wounded for our transgressions,
He was bruised for our iniquities;
The chastisement for our peace was upon Him,
And by His stripes we are healed. (Isaiah 53:5)(NKJV)

<u>Wounded for our transgressions</u>: We have sinned, we are guilty before God.

<u>Bruised for our iniquities</u>: He was our substitute! He took our punishment and paid for our sins.

<u>The chastisement of our peace was upon Him</u> (Rom 5:1) tells us we are justified by faith, peach with God through Jesus Christ.

<u>With His stripes we are healed:</u> through salvation we are physically and spiritually healed.

Sickness and disease started with the fall of man (Adam and Eve) due to disobedience in the garden. As a result, sin separated us from God. But... Jesus reconciled us once again.

- He was wounded... (we were guilty) ...confess sin
- He was bruised... (for our past mistakes) ...Be honest, come clean
- Our peace is in Him... (when the guilt is gone because our wrongs are done away- we have peace) ...accept His freedom

WHEN YOU KNOW YOU ARE IN RIGHT RELATIONSHIP
WITH GOD YOU CAN BELIEVE HIM FOR ANYTHING!

No more: guilt, stress, worry.... FREEDOM!

Healing: in the mind, emotions, spiritually, THE REST FOLLOWS!

Lord Jesus, I know I have fallen short, I am sorry; I need a new touch from you. Please forgive me and come into my life and be my Lord as well as my Savior. Thank you, Jesus, for never giving up on me and I now know that I have the VICTORY IN JESUS!

January 13

THE ROCK

...having been built on the foundation of the apostles and prophets, Jesus Christ Himself being the chief cornerstone, (Ephesians 2:20) (NKJV)

In Bible times buildings were made of cut, squared stone. By uniting two intersecting walls, a cornerstone helped align the whole building and tie it together.

When Moses was fighting the Amalekites he sat on a stone, "rock".

Christ Jesus "The Rock" is the one who aligns our life and keeps it together. When tired or fighting a battle, rest upon "The Rock"

Oh Lord, no matter what I am facing today, I know as you help me to trust you, I know my life will be aligned properly and in my weary times I will rest in you, "my Rock" I will sit and listen to your *still small voice*.

January 14

BLESSING –VS– GLORY

Paul and Timothy, bondservants of Jesus Christ,
To all the saints in Christ Jesus who are in Philippi, with
the bishops and deacons: Grace to you and peace from God
our Father and the Lord Jesus Christ.
I thank my God upon every remembrance of you, always in every prayer
of mine making request for you all with joy, for your fellowship in the
gospel from the first day until now, being confident of this very thing,
that He who has begun a good work in you will complete it until the
day of Jesus Christ; just as it is right for me to think this of you all,
because I have you in my heart, inasmuch as both in my chains and
in the defense and confirmation of the gospel, you all are partakers
with me of grace. For God is my witness, how greatly I long for you
all with the affection of Jesus Christ. And this I pray, that your love may
abound still more and more in knowledge and all discernment, that you
may approve the things that are excellent, that you may be sincere and
without offense till the day of Christ, (Philippians 3:1-10) (NKJV)

Paul's greatest burden was that people were being led astray.

Are we looking for the blessing or God's glory? Don't get caught up in programs, manifestations or wild worship. When Jesus rode into town He cleaned the temple and said His house would be a house of prayer. Don't be concerned with what's going on instead of (who) is taking care of you. Jesus said He'd never leave you or forsake you.

• Seek God's glory and the blessings will follow.

January 15

PROMISES WE CAN STAND ON TO MAKE IT

Have you not known?
Have you not heard?
The everlasting God, the LORD,
The Creator of the ends of the earth,
Neither faints nor is weary.
His understanding is unsearchable.
He gives power to the weak,
And to those who have no might He increases strength.
Even the youths shall faint and be weary,
And the young men shall utterly fall,
But those who wait on the LORD
Shall renew their strength;
They shall mount up with wings like eagles,
They shall run and not be weary,
They shall walk and not faint. (Isaiah 40:28-31)(NKJV)

Waiting is to trust God fully with our lives.
God promises you:

- Strength
- To rise above your difficulties
- To run spiritually without quitting
- To walk, continue on without fainting

YOU ARE NEVER ALONE!

Fear not, for I am with you; Be not dismayed, for I am your God.
I will strengthen you, Yes, I will help you,
I will uphold you with My righteous right hand.
(Isaiah 41:10)(NKJV)

- Wait
- Trust God fully

January 16

TEARS OF MY HEART

Then one of the Pharisees asked Him to eat with him. And He went to the Pharisee's house, and sat down to eat. And behold, a woman in the city who was a sinner, when she knew that Jesus sat at the table in the Pharisee's house, brought an alabaster flask of fragrant oil, and stood at His feet behind Him weeping; and she began to wash His feet with her tears, and wiped them with the hair of her head; and she kissed His feet and anointed them with the fragrant oil. (Luke 7:36-38)(NKJV)

Here is a woman with an unclean, disrespected reputation and yet Jesus accepted her. The Pharisee looking on accused Jesus of not being a prophet for if He was, He would have known this woman's reputation and forbidden her to touch Him. She washed the dusty, tired feet of Jesus with her tears, wiped them with the hair on her head and anointed them with very expensive oil. Her tears flowed physically from her face, but emotionally they were triggered by her repentive, worshipful, loving adoring heart towards a man (a Savior) of great love and acceptance. For once in her life someone accepted her for who she is and not for what they can get from her. That is the Savior's love.

We have all been there, we have all needed a Savior...someone who would accept us, hold us, forgive us, comfort us and let us know that we are His very own and He will love us, protect us and care for us, that He will never leave us alone but hold us close to His bosom. That is our Lord and Savior Jesus Christ. No one will ever love you like Jesus. Oh no, the woman did not wash Jesus feet with the tears from her face, but tears of her heart.

Remember the love that He had for you when He gave Himself on Calvary. You can have that inner assurance that you are forgiven and cared for. God knows there are times of weakness and He does not kick us when we are down. Tears are not only on our face, but real repentance is tears of our heart.

January 17

FOOL OR FREE?

Moreover, He said to me, "Son of man, eat what you find;
eat this scroll, and go, speak to the house of Israel." So, I
opened my mouth, and He caused me to eat that scroll.
And He said to me, "Son of man, feed your belly, and fill your
stomach with this scroll that I give you." So I ate, and it was in
my mouth like honey in sweetness. (Ezekiel 3:1-3)(NKJV)

God gave Ezekiel a prophetic ministry. In receiving a vision from God's glory and throne he was called to deliver a message from the Lord of judgment to Judah and Jerusalem. The scroll was the words from God for His people. Ezekiel's eating it symbolized that he had to receive it himself and commit to proclaiming it. Although he was bringing a message of warning and destruction God caused it to be as sweet as honey to the prophet. God's Word will be loved and valued by all who are committed to Him. As the song says: "I Am Desperate for You."[22]

Don't be a fool like those in Judah and Jerusalem. Don't go your own way... be committed to God and "be free." Are you desperate for Him?

The scroll...that *still small voice*

January 18

I WILL MAKE IT!

Brethren, I do not count myself to have apprehended; but one thing I do, forgetting those things which are behind and reaching forward to those things which are ahead, I press toward the goal for the prize of the upward call of God in Christ Jesus. (Philippians 3:13-14)(NKJV)

Paul is saying that he has not yet arrived but he cannot hold onto his past failures because there is something so great ahead.

- Don't worry about anything
- Pray about everything

A song my boys used to sing when they were younger goes like this:

Mighty warrior, Dressed for battle
Holy Lord of All is He. Commander and chief
Bring us to attention
Lead us into battle, to crush the enemy

Satan has no authority here in this place
He has no authority here. For this habitation
Was fashioned for the Lord's presence
No authority here![33]

God has called you to be a warrior; a mighty warrior. You are a warrior because you are in a battle: the battle is for your soul and the souls in your family. A battle is not easy but do you want to win?

- Keep your eyes on the prize
- You WILL make it!

January 19

"GO FORWARD"

And Moses said to the people, "Do not be afraid. Stand still, and
see the salvation of the Lord, which He will accomplish for you
today. For the Egyptians whom you see today, you shall see again no
more forever. The Lord will fight for you, and you shall hold your
peace." And the Lord said to Moses, "Why do you cry to Me? Tell
the children of Israel to go forward. (Exodus 14:13-15)(NKJV)

Finally, after many plagues Pharaoh angrily agreed to let Moses take the
Israelites out of Egypt where they had been bound in slavery for many
years. Here they are in front of the Red Sea, they cried to Moses; knowing
that the angry Pharaoh must be on their trail and now they are in front
of the sea. Obviously, they could not go around it or through it (so they
thought). The Lord in a sense chastised Moses in saying; "why do you cry
to me?" After all, didn't they experience for themselves how powerful
their great Jehovah was? He has been their shield of protection. While the
Egyptians were suffering from the plagues the Israelites were unharmed.

God told Moses to "go forward." He knew they were facing a fast sea that
could not be crossed, why would He tell them to go forward? God did not
bring them this far to leave them!

• If in the face of the sea if you are told to "go" then "go."

As they proceeded, much to their amazement they began to experience the
power and strength of their mighty God. The roar of the waves flushed
to one side and then to the other...my goodness...God had made a path
directly through the humongous body of water. They marched through

on dry ground, a wall of water on each side. God brought them through dry, unharmed and hallelujah...they were free! Look at God!

- If God tells you to go forward ...go forward.
- He is the God who can part the waters!
- Is your problem bigger than the Red Sea?

January 20

LET IT GO

But now you yourselves are to put off all these: anger, wrath, malice, blasphemy, filthy language out of your mouth. Do not lie to one another, since you have put off the old man with his deeds, and have put on the new man who is renewed in knowledge according to the image of Him who created him (Colossians 3:8-10)(NKJV)

If I were to put clear nail polish on my nails they would look really good. However, if I continually put it on week after week never taking it off, my nails would become dry, yellow and crack. Oh, they would look good for a good long time but after a while the results would not be so appealing. Similar is what we do when we cover things up.

Have you been hurt by someone, maybe your husband, wife, mother, father, sister, brother, etc.? Feels like a split in the relationship? Your feelings are soft or sensitive, your heart is cracking? Is it taking so much out of you that you feel like you're being stripped of your rights? Do you feel that as a person you are being peeled like an onion until you become what someone else wants you to be?

The colder you get the easier it is to stay hard. Like the clear nail polish, you will look good for a while but after a period of time, you will not look so good, dry up and eventually crack. THAT DOES NOT NEED TO HAPPEN!

- Give it to God
- Tell Him how you feel

Ask yourself: Does this affect my salvation?

The thicker the coating, the harder it is to rub off. It may not be overnight but:

- Get in your Bible. It is not over...the Bible says that God takes the foolish things of this world to confound the wise.
- LET IT GO!

Listen to His *still small voice*.

January 21

FROM GLORY TO GLORY

But we all, with unveiled face, beholding as in a mirror the glory of the Lord, are being transformed into the same image from glory to glory, just as by the Spirit of the Lord. (II Corinthians 3:18)(NKJV)

Has your veil been fear of someone finding out who you really are or were? Or maybe guilt for what you've done, deep hurt or unforgiveness because of what's been done to you? Something you're trying to hide or forget as if it never happened? Fear, guilt, and hurt…it is all bondage.

Experience God's glory…no you are not worthy, no one is but He forgives anyway…BECAUSE HE LOVES YOU!

Look at all the Lord has really done for you…know you can let it go! See Him for who He really is and experience His glory! Then you are on the road from glory to glory.

- Be honest – let it go!
- Confess it to God, don't hide it
- Let it go and be free!

From glory to glory means to behold the truth and person of Jesus Christ, to experience His nearness, His love and His power through prayer. It is knowing the magnitude of who He really is.

- Pray
- Talk to Him
- Have an encounter with Jesus

Listen to His *still small voice*

January 22

WAIT

Be still, and know that I am God;
I will be exalted among the nations,
I will be exalted in the earth! (Psalm 46:10)(NKJV)

The song says:

> We must wait, wait, wait on the Lord
> We must wait, wait, wait on the Lord
> Learn this lesson well
> In His timing He will tell us
> What to do
> Where to go
> What to say
> Wait on the Lord.[44]

- Don't do anything until you have prayed
- Watch God be God!

January 23

NEW LIFE

Blessed be the God and Father of our Lord Jesus Christ, who according to His abundant mercy has begotten us again to a living hope through the resurrection of Jesus Christ from the dead (I Peter 1:3)(NKJV)

God has given us "new life" born again and a "living hope" because Jesus is alive, so is our hope. If Jesus conquered death what can we hope for?

- Alive Christ – alive faith!

He conquered the ultimate so our faith should be the ultimate.

- Nothing is too big for God!

January 24

HEARERS –VS– DOERS

Now I would not have you ignorant, brethren, that oftentimes I
purposed to come unto you, (but was let hitherto,) that I might
have some fruit among you also, even as among other Gentiles
(Romans 1:13)(NKJV)

From vs. 1-15 Paul was writing to the Romans for he had heard how they were living and since the church was started under his ministry he bore a responsibility to them. He heard they were not living the same gospel he had preached. The same gospel they were converted under and the gospel on which the church had been started. There was more to life than money, fun and fellowship.

God wants us to be doers not just hearers alone. Maybe you find yourself in that place but remember:

- It's in the desert that the dew is the freshest and the air is the purest.
- Listen to His *still small voice*
- And "DO IT!"

January 25

A TIME AND A SEASON

To everything there is a season, and a time to every purpose under the heaven: A time to be born, and a time to die; a time to plant, and a time to pluck up that which is planted; A time to kill, and a time to heal; a time to break down, and a time to build up; A time to weep, and a time to laugh; a time to mourn, and a time to dance; A time to cast away stones, and a time to gather stones together; a time to embrace, and a time to refrain from embracing; A time to get, and a time to lose; a time to keep, and a time to cast away; A time to rend, and a time to sew; a time to keep silence, and a time to speak; A time to love, and a time to hate; a time of war, and a time of peace (Ecclesiastes 3:1-8)(NKJV)

Solomon was a man of wealth, power, honor, fame…he had it all in abundance, yet in the end found it all to be emptiness. He wanted to share in Ecclesiastes his regrets and personal testimony. Solomon was the son of King David and describes himself as the wisest ruler of God's people. Yet his spiritual decline was because of idolatry and a life of self-indulgence. Ultimately, he was left disillusioned with pleasure and materialism as a way to happiness.

Don't give up if you are in a "time or season"

- Put the Lord first
- Satisfy Him

You will reap eternal joy, happiness and life.

January 26

STRONG BUT GOOD

For I know the thoughts that I think toward you, saith the LORD,
thoughts of peace, and not of evil, to give you an expected end
(Jeremiah 29:11)(NKJV)

Jeremiah was known as the weeping prophet because of the burden in his heart for his people. Seeing the sin of Judah and Israel, God sent Jeremiah to warn them. He preached mostly judgment and some restoration. Unfortunately, it seemed that the prophesies fell on deaf ears. However, because of God being the God of another chance that He is, He was telling the people that He has a good plan for their lives. The key was they must stop doing things their way and begin serving God.

Although Jeremiah brought a strong word from the Lord, it was a well needed one. If we are not corrected, how will we turn around? You may have turned to your own ways and find yourself struggling to get back on course.

Remember: God has a plan and a future for you. He's not given up on you.

Listen for His *still small voice.*

January 27

PRACTICAL LIVING

But God hath chosen the foolish things of the world to confound the wise; and God hath chosen the weak things of the world to confound the things which are mighty (I Corinthians 1:27) (KJV)

<u>Coca Cola</u>

A pharmacist from Georgia made something that would relieve exhaustion and sooth headaches. He told his assistant to add water and chill it with ice but the second time he made a mistake, he added carbonated water. Instead of selling it as a headache remedy, it was sold as a fountain drink.

Chocolate chip cookies, potato chips...they were all mistakes that were turned around and made good. We've all made mistakes in our lives but (when we trust God) only He can turn them around for our good. He will use your mistakes to help you to live practically. It's not so terrible to make a mistake; it's making it over and over again and never learning from it. The Lord will help you to learn from your mistake and what the devil meant for evil God will turn around for you.

- Stop
- It's not too late
- Obey His *still small voice*

January 28

STAND

Finally, my brethren, be strong in the Lord and in the power of His might. Put on the whole armor of God, that you may be able to stand against the wiles of the devil. For we do not wrestle against flesh and blood, but against principalities, against powers, against the rulers of the darkness of this age, against spiritual hosts of wickedness in the heavenly places. Therefore take up the whole armor of God, that you may be able to withstand in the evil day, and having done all, to stand. Stand therefore, having girded your waist with truth, having put on the breastplate of righteousness, and having shod your feet with the preparation of the gospel of peace; above all, taking the shield of faith with which you will be able to quench all the fiery darts of the wicked one. And take the helmet of salvation, and the sword of the Spirit, which is the word of God; praying always with all prayer and supplication in the Spirit, being watchful to this end with all perseverance and supplication for all the saints.
(Ephesians 6:10-18) (NKJV)

Stand:

- To <u>be</u> or <u>remain</u> in an <u>upright</u> position.
- To rise to an <u>upright</u> position.
- To take, <u>maintain</u> or be in a position, <u>attitude</u> or course.
- To <u>remain</u> where situated
- To <u>remain</u> <u>unchanged</u>
- To <u>maintain</u> one's viewpoint, or opinion
- To <u>remain</u> <u>firm</u>

We are not fighting one another. Do not let earthly feelings or circumstances affect your relationship with God.

- If God said it, that's all there is to it

Your victory has been secured by Jesus Christ through His death on the cross.

Lord, I take the authority that you have invested in me on the cross at Calvary, In the Name of Jesus...

- We are in warfare!
- When God has you on hold, don't hang up

January 29

THE WHOLE ARMOR OF GOD

I Samuel Chapter 17...read it!

David fought Goliath in "full armor". All Goliath saw was a slingshot, but David's armor was there by faith, coming from years of godly discipline while in the wilderness caring for his sheep.

The enemy will do his best to keep you from God's Word because he knows that is where your power will come from and ultimately you will KNOW that you have the victory. Satan will look at you with just a slingshot, but you will KNOW that your fully clothed and ready for battle with a force behind you that is not your own.

- Read the Word!

January 30

BELT OF TRUTH

Stand therefore, having girded your waist with truth, having put on the breastplate of righteousness, (Ephesians 6:14)(NKJV)

In Biblical times soldiers wore clothes that reached the floor and when they needed to run they would pick up the bottom and tuck it into their "belt"

• Another name for truth is FREEDOM!

Then Jesus said to those Jews who believed Him, "If you abide in My Word, you are my disciples indeed. And you shall know the truth, and the truth shall make you free." (John 8: 31-32)(NKJV)

January 31

BREASTPLATE OF RIGHTEOUSNESS

*Stand therefore, having girded your waist with truth, having put
on the breastplate of righteousness, (Ephesians 6:14)(NKJV)*

The breastplate protected vital organs.

*Your word I have hidden in my heart,
That I might not sin against You. (Psalm 119:11)(NKJV)*

• READ THE WORD OF GOD!

February 1

FEET SHOD WITH THE
GOSPEL OF PEACE

*And having shod your feet with the preparation of the gospel
of peace; (Ephesians 6:15)(NKJV)*

The foot is a symbol of authority. In Bible times when a king was conquered he was brought to the ruler. He'd bow his head to the floor and the victorious ruler would put his foot on the neck of his defeated foe.

KNOW WHO YOUR GOD IS AND THAT YOUR STRENGTH IS IN HIM!

February 2

SHIELD OF FAITH

Above all, taking the shield of faith with which you will be
able to quench all the fiery darts of the wicked one.
(Ephesians 6:16)(NKJV)

The shield would protect against the enemy's blows. Each soldier's shield would lock together with another soldier's thus creating a wall, which made them stronger in battle.

FASTING: LOCKING FAITH WITH GOD

February 3

HELMET OF SALVATION

And take the helmet of salvation, (Ephesians 6:17a)(NKJV)

A soldier's helmet was the most important part of his armor because if the enemy hit his head it would disable him. Satan tries to get us through our minds through fear. Fear will get our minds off the power of God and who He is.

He who dwells in the secret place of the Most High
Shall abide under the shadow of the Almighty.
I will say of the LORD, "He is my refuge and my fortress;
My God, in Him I will trust." (Psalm 91:1-2)(NKJV)

KNOW YOUR GOD IS WHO HE SAYS HE IS AND HE'S NOT A MAN THAT HE SHOULD LIE!

February 4

SWORD OF THE SPIRIT

And the sword of the Spirit, which is the word of God ;
(Ephesians 6:17b)(NKJV)

<u>The sword is the first offensive weapon.</u> A good sword was two edged so the soldier could wield it at the enemy in any direction. That is why we need the Word of God "Rhema" direct word from the Holy Spirit.

HAVE YOU READ THE WORD OF GOD TODAY?

February 5

PRAYER

Praying always with all prayer and supplication in the Spirit,
being watchful to this end with all perseverance and supplication
for all the saints—and for me, that utterance may be given
to me, that I may open my mouth boldly to make known
the mystery of the gospel (Ephesians 6:18-19)(NKJV)

Prayer is the second offensive weapon. Make known the mystery of the
Gospel.

- Don't be ashamed of the Gospel
- It's your weapon
- Know it well!

February 6

TAKE AUTHORITY!

For the past few days you have been reading about the armor of God, now apply it.

1. KNOW THE TRUTH
2. HIDE THE WORD IN YOUR HEART
3. KNOW YOU HAVE AUTHORITY (PEACE)
4. FIGHT THE ATTACKS (FAITH)
5. KNOW YOU ARE SAVED! (SECURITY)
6. GET INTO THE WORD
7. FIGHT WITH THE WORD OF GOD
8. PRAY!

February 7

RECEIVING OUR INHERITANCE

Wives, likewise, be submissive to your own husbands, that even if
some do not obey the Word, they, without a word, may be won by
the conduct of their wives, when they observe your chaste conduct
accompanied by fear. Do not let your adornment be merely outward—
arranging the hair, wearing gold, or putting on fine apparel—rather
let it be the hidden person of the heart, with the incorruptible beauty
of a gentle and quiet spirit, which is very precious in the sight of God.
For in this manner, in former times, the holy women who trusted in
God also adorned themselves, being submissive to their own husbands,
as Sarah obeyed Abraham, calling him lord, whose daughters you are
if you do good and are not afraid with any terror. Husbands, likewise,
dwell with them with understanding, giving honor to the wife, as to
the weaker vessel, and as being heirs together of the grace of life, that
your prayers may not be hindered. Finally, all of you be of one mind,
having compassion for one another; love as brothers, be tenderhearted,
be courteous; 9not returning evil for evil or reviling for reviling, but on
the contrary blessing, knowing that you were called to this, that you may
inherit a blessing. For "He who would love life And see good days,
Let him refrain his tongue from evil,
And his lips from speaking deceit.
Let him turn away from evil and do good;
Let him seek peace and pursue it.
For the eyes of the Lord are on the righteous,
And His ears are open to their prayers;
And who is he who will harm you if you become followers of what is
good? But even if you should suffer for righteousness' sake, you
But the face of the Lord is against those who do evil."
are blessed. "And do not be afraid of their threats, nor be troubled.

"But sanctify the Lord God in your hearts, and always be ready to give a defense to everyone who asks you a reason for the hope that is in you, with meekness and fear; having a good conscience, that when they defame you as evildoers, those who revile your good conduct in Christ may be ashamed. (I Peter 3:1-16)(NKJV)

You may be going through a rough time but hold on, there's a blessing coming. Just be concerned with keeping yourself clean. We are royalty, but we still have to obey rules. Submit to those who rule over you – employer, teacher, parent, etc.

Have respect so the heathen will see God at work in your life.

February 8

(CONTINUED FROM FEB 7)

Wives

Don't seek outward beauty but inward. Be of a meek and quiet spirit.

Meekness: An attitude of <u>humility</u> toward God and <u>gentleness</u> toward people, springing from the recognition <u>that God</u> <u>is in control</u>.

Quiet spirit: Not easily agitated or disturbed, a quiet and peaceful attitude.

- True beauty is a matter of character not devotion

Husbands

1. Be <u>considerate</u> and <u>understanding</u> with an intelligent recognition of the marriage relation.
2. Respect her as physically weaker. (<u>Protect and provide</u>)
3. Realize that God has put you together because of His grace.

The Bible tells us that a man, who finds a wife, finds a good thing. It wasn't good for man to be alone so God created Eve.

Otherwise…Your prayers will be cut off, causing you to not pray effectively. You will damage your relationship with God by creating a barrier between your prayers and God.

- Don't do it!
- Follow God's law and receive your inheritance
- Is it hard….? Listen to hear His ***still small voice***

February 9

CREATING AN ATMOSPHERE
FOR GOD

Then the LORD said to Moses, "Go to the people and consecrate them
today and tomorrow, and let them wash their clothes. And let them be
ready for the third day. For on the third day the LORD will come down
upon Mount Sinai in the sight of all the people. You shall set bounds for
the people all around, saying, 'Take heed to yourselves that you do not go
up to the mountain or touch its base. Whoever touches the mountain shall
surely be put to death. Not a hand shall touch Him, but he shall surely
be stoned or shot with an arrow; whether man or beast, he shall not live.'
When the trumpet sounds long, they shall come near the mountain."
(Exodus 19:10-13)(NKJV)

The Lord was directing Moses on what to say to the people preparing them
to hear from God.

- Don't just approach God like anyone else… (Know He is holy!)
- Wait for God's voice
- Don't have anything on your mind but Him

Why?

- To demonstrate the awesome Power and Holiness of God.
- To build Moses' faith and to establish Moses' authority
- To establish fear in the hearts of the people so they will not sin
- To make know to the people that disobedience to God's Word
  would result in death.

Do you want to hear from God? Listen to His *still small voice.*

February 10

HIS MERCY NEVER ENDS

Oh, give thanks to the Lord, for He is good!
For His mercy endures forever.
Oh, give thanks to the God of gods!
For His mercy endures forever.
Oh, give thanks to the Lord of lords!
For His mercy endures forever:
To Him who alone does great wonders,
For His mercy endures forever;
To Him who by wisdom made the heavens,
For His mercy endures forever;
To Him who laid out the earth above the waters,
For His mercy endures forever;
To Him who made great lights,
For His mercy endures forever—
The sun to rule by day,
For His mercy endures forever;
The moon and stars to rule by night,
For His mercy endures forever.
To Him who struck Egypt in their firstborn,
For His mercy endures forever;
And brought out Israel from among them,
For His mercy endures forever;
With a strong hand, and with an outstretched arm,
For His mercy endures forever;
To Him who divided the Red Sea in two,
For His mercy endures forever;
And made Israel pass through the midst of it,
For His mercy endures forever;

But overthrew Pharaoh and his army in the Red Sea,
For His mercy endures forever;
To Him who led His people through the wilderness,
For His mercy endures forever;
To Him who struck down great kings,
For His mercy endures forever;
And slew famous kings,
For His mercy endures forever—
Sihon king of the Amorites,
For His mercy endures forever;
And Og king of Bashan,
For His mercy endures forever—
And gave their land as a heritage,
For His mercy endures forever;
A heritage to Israel His servant,
For His mercy endures forever.
Who remembered us in our lowly state,
For His mercy endures forever;
And rescued us from our enemies,
For His mercy endures forever;
Who gives food to all flesh,
For His mercy endures forever.
Oh, give thanks to the God of heaven! (Psalm 136:1-26)(NKJV)

- Even when we don't think so
- Even when we don't know it
- Even when we don't feel it
- Even when we don't deserve it
- Even when we don't see it
- Even in the storm
- Even in the confusion
- Even in the trials
- Even in the mistakes
- Even in the hurts
- Even in the lean times
- Even in the times of blessing
- Even in the impossible times
- Even in the Red Sea times

February 11

(CONTINUED FROM FEB 10)

- Even in the times of triumph
- Even in the times of fear
- Even in the times of weakness
- Even in the times of torment
- Even in the times of weariness
- Even in the times of heartache
- Even in the times of battle
- Even in the times of uncertainty
- Even in the times of loneliness
- He was merciful yesterday
- He's merciful today
- He'll be merciful tomorrow

You've NEVER gone too far from His mercy.

- His mercy is for you
- His mercy is for me
- His mercy is not earned
- His mercy is not deserved
- His mercy is just given

Because His mercy endures forever.

Why don't you thank Him for His mercies that He's bestowed on you?

THANK YOU!!!! I LOVE YOU JESUS!!!

February 12

BECAUSE HE TOUCHED ME

One generation shall praise Your works to another,
And shall declare Your mighty acts (Psalm 145:4)(NKJV)

Psalms are either prayers or praises. They were Israel's hymns. David is praising God for His greatness. How can generation after generation praise Him? Because of an experience.

- What has God done in your life?
- Has He been there in times no one else was?
- Did He come through for you when you didn't know what to do?
- Has He proved Himself to be faithful?

Israel praised God because of their experience with Him. If you look back and as the old song says: "Count your blessings, name them one by one." [5] They would be too numerous for you to count. There are situations the Lord saved you from that you are not even aware of.

- He has been your provider
- He satisfies

Who is the next generation to praise Him? Could it be your children? Forsake the feelings of doubt and despair, look around you, see what the Lord has done and feelings or not "PRAISE HIM!"

---

[5] *Count Your Blessings*, Words by Rev. Johnson Oatman, Jr., Music by Edwin O. Excell, 1897, Public Domain

Why? He touched your life! Where would you be without the Lord?
PRAISE HIM! Because...HE TOUCHED YOU!

> Great is they faithfulness
> Great is thy faithfulness
> Morning by morning new mercies I see
> All I have needed thy hand hath provided
> Great is thy faithfulness
> Great is thy faithfulness
> Great is thy faithfulness
> Lord unto me[6]

★ ★ ★

The wood in the stove is crackling; I look out the six panel windows to
see soft flakes of snow quietly falling from the heavenlies. The beauty of
it all...surely.... I can say... great is my God's faithfulness.

You know, problems could be all around you, but take the time to be still...
look around you and see that He is God.

---

[6] *Great Is Thy Faithfulness*, Words by Thomas O. Chisholm, Music by
William M. Runyan, 1923, Public Domain.

February 13

WHAT IS YOUR DREAM? GO FOR IT!

But Jesus looked at them and said to them, "With men this
is impossible, but with God all things are possible."
(Matthew 19:26) (NKJV)

This text is often times taken out of context. Someone came to Jesus asking what he must do to acquire eternal life. Jesus answers his question with the commandments and the person continues on at which time Jesus responds by telling him that he should sell all he has and give it to the poor. The person then leaves sadly and Jesus continues on to say in verses 29 – 30.

And everyone who has left houses or brothers or sisters or father
or mother or wife or children or lands, for My name's sake, shall
receive a hundredfold, and inherit eternal life. But many who are
first will be last, and the last first. (Matthew 19:29-30)(NKJV)

Jesus is actually saying that our motives are to be for Him and His glory. PUT HIM FIRST!

- What is your dream?
- Why do you want it?
- Who will receive glory from it?

Don't give up on your dream, put Jesus first and watch what happens.

February 14

LONGING FOR THE BRIDEGROOM

Set me as a seal upon your heart,
As a seal upon your arm;
For love is as strong as death,
Jealousy as cruel as the grave;
Its flames are flames of fire,
A most vehement flame. (Song of Solomon 8:6)(NKJV)

The Song of Solomon is a poem – a song inspired by the Holy Spirit to underscore the divine origin of the joy and dignity of human love in marriage. It's the only book in the Bible that deals exclusively with the unique love of a bride and bridegroom. It's a song about Solomon and the Shulamite woman.

The Shulamite woman is in love with Solomon, they are planning to get married, but they are not yet. How they are longing for each other. She is longing for her groom to be, desiring his kiss, his fragrance, their time alone. Solomon assures her that she can have all he has. She lures him with her perfume and speaks of her longing for him. Solomon responds with words of the same, assuring her of his love for her. "Oh, how handsome you are" the Shulamite woman feverishly whispers; she tells him of her beauty. Solomon brings her home and longs for her beauty but he cannot have her. They are longing for each other but they must wait.

"The Wedding"
A large wedding, the dust of the procession mingled with perfumes and powders. Sixty handpicked escorts, Solomon's couch arrayed with silver and gold with a purple cushion signifying wealth and royalty adorned

with beautiful flowers while cheering women singing & dancing. What a celebration!

With longing in his eyes Solomon looks upon his bride. He sees her eyes behind the veil, her lips, face, temples, he longs for her body. He longs to be alone with her, smell her fragrance...she's spotless!

Solomon: "you've won my heart, just a little move of your necklace, your lips, and your perfume." The woman is saying, "Come to me, and enjoy me."

The scripture says: love is as strong as death; its flames are like flames of fire...

- Water cannot quench love - floods cannot drown love.

The Shulamite woman is saying; here I am, take me and Solomon is hanging on the sound of her voice

- When was the last time you desired your bridegroom in such a way?
- Are you hungry for the Savior's love?
- For His touch, His voice?

He's coming back for you, are you longing for His appearing?

- Spend time with Him
- Have you heard His *still small voice* ?

February 15

HAPPY BIRTHDAY SALVATORE!

Salvatore
Meaning: Savior

Today is my first grandson Salvatore's birthday. He is the boy with gusto! Since Sal was two years old I nicknamed him "the bullet" as I saw the speed and endurance he had as a runner. Today he plays football, baseball, basketball, and has wrestled. He's a star player (shhh, can't show favoritism... ha-ha). This boy runs so fast that unless he is tackled from the side no one behind can catch him. I have since named him "Secretariat" as there is no race horse in history that has ever come close or attempted his record.

Sal is loving, kind and compassionate. I love it when he wraps his arms around my neck and kisses me, but one thing that is so very special is that he truly loves Jesus with all his heart. He is tender towards the things of God and is sincerely concerned for those who aren't. He loves his family and no matter how old he gets I believe he will always have that little boy inside of him who likes to be hugged, caressed and sung to. I love you Salvatore Nicholas and pray that God will always keep you safe, make you the head and not the tail, always the winner and never a loser...you are God's gift to our family and this Nonna loves you more than words can express. You are more than anyone could ever ask for! God bless you Secretariat!

Can I challenge you today to bless someone?

February 16

TRUST RESULTS IN BLESSING

My son, do not forget my law,
But let your heart keep my commands;
For length of days and long life
And peace they will add to you.
Let not mercy and truth forsake you;
Bind them around your neck,
Write them on the tablet of your heart,
And so find favor and high esteem (Proverbs 3:1-2)(NKJV)

Trust in the LORD with all your heart,
And lean not on your own understanding;
In all your ways acknowledge Him,
And He shall direct your paths. (Proverbs 3:5-6)(NKJV)

Keep the law/commandments of God and there are three promises of God in this Psalm. (Read it)

- He will stretch your days and extend your life. (a quality day)
- Long life, (health and provision)
- Peace

Never forget what the Lord has done for you, stay sweet and humble. Know where your strength, health and provision come from.

- Trust God with and for everything
- Never mind what you think
- Acknowledge God in everything in your life.

Don't take credit – let God be God!

February 17

VISION

Where there is no vision, the people perish: (Prov. 29:18) (KJV)

Vision: the act or power of seeing with the eye, sense or sight.

How hard is it for God to save a soul, deliver from drugs, alcohol or life controlling bondages? Again, I ask you; how hard is it for God? Too often we carry burdens and worry about things needlessly. Is God, God? Is there anything too hard for Him? Why are you trying to do it yourself? God understands, He knows and what's more important is He knew it would happen before it even did.

I don't care who it is you are burdened for, your son, daughter, spouse. You cannot save them but in KNOWING who God is you've got to KNOW that He is not only willing but able to do it. In KNOWING that, start praising Him for the answer. Envision the completed work; start acting as if it already has taken place.

- See it
- Sense it
- Know it is done

February 18

FIRE OF GOD

Then the fire of the Lord fell and consumed the burnt sacrifice, and the wood and the stones and the dust, and t It licked up the water that was in the trench. Now when all the people saw it, they fell on their faces; and they said, "The Lord, He is God! The Lord, He is God!" (I Kings 18:38-39)(NKJV)

Elijah was challenging the prophets of Baal to call on their God and see who is really God. They built an altar and called on their god but nothing was happening. When it came time for Elijah to call on his god, He truly did respond in power and majesty! The fire of God consumed everything on the altar.

Let the fire of God:

Burn up your sins, inconsistencies, and things that keep you from growing in Him.

Nothing will burn it but the "fire of God!" Show the devil and this world that the "fire of God" **IS** greater than any worldly power. It's the "fire of God" that will change your life.

Kindling:

- Reading the Word of God
- Spending time in His presence
- Fasting
- Praying
- Listening to His ***still small voice***

February 19

PRAISE AND WORSHIP
(PART ONE)

It is good to give thanks to the Lord,
And to sing praises to Your name, O Most High ;
(Psalm 92:1)(NKJV)

Read:

Psalm 95:1-2
Psalm 98:1,4,5,6
Psalm 100:1,2,4
Psalm 111:1
Psalm 112:1
Psalm 113:1,3
Psalm 117:1,2
Psalm 135:1,3
Psalm 139:14
Psalm 146:1,2
Psalm 147:1,7,12,20
Psalm 148:1-5,7,13,14
Psalm 149:1,3,9
Psalm 150:1-6

(Everyone talks about praising Him)

PRAISE HIM!

February 20

PRAISE AND WORSHIP
(PART TWO)

But the hour is coming, and now is, when the true worshipers
will worship the Father in spirit and truth; for the Father
is seeking such to worship Him. God is Spirit, and those
who worship Him must worship in spirit and truth."
(John 4:23-24)(NKJV)

Praise is a physical activity while worship on the other hand is a spiritual thing. You can teach someone to praise but you cannot teach someone to worship. Praise is a physical activity towards God in response to what He has done. Worship is pure sincere adoration.

Are you praising Him or worshiping Him?

Worshiping Him in spirit and in truth is a lifestyle. We glorify God by our actions, speech and how we live. It is hard for all of us through different trials of life but the only way to live in such way is when facing the hard to handle moments…take time out to listen to His *still small voice.*

February 21

ELEMENTS OF WORSHIP

Speaking to one another in psalms and hymns and spiritual songs, singing and making melody in your heart to the Lord, giving thanks always for all things to God the Father in the name of our Lord Jesus Christ, (Ephesians 5:19-20)(NKJV)

- Singing hymns and spiritual songs
- Seeking God's face in prayer
- Confession of sins
- Tithes and offerings

Are you singing to God in thanksgiving for not only what He has done but for Who He is?

- How much time do you have for Him?
- Have you confessed your sins?
- Are you faithful to God's Word?

We have all fallen short of what is expected of us. Aren't we glad we have a Heavenly Father who loves us and does not kick us when we are down? That is why we worship Him…because He loves us.

February 22

MANIFESTATIONS OF WORSHIP

For where two or three are gathered together in My name, I am there in the midst of them." (Matthew 18:20)(NKJV)

When God shows up, something is going to happen! He does not show up to give us goose bumps. In His presence ANYTHING can happen and ANYTHING WILL HAPPEN!

His Holy Spirit begins to work and any number of ways:

- Word of wisdom
- Word of knowledge
- Gifts of healing
- Working of miracles
- Prophecy
- Discernment
- Speaking in tongues
- Interpretation of tongues

When was the last time you have experienced the Holy Spirit at work in your situation?

WORSHIP JESUS!

February 24

FIRE OF GOD

Therefore submit to God. Resist the devil and he
will flee from you. (James 4:7)(NKJV)

Privileged to be a speaker for a Missionette Powette I sat near a great bonfire. As the fire burned, sparks flew in the air. The Holy Spirit began to birth a message about the sparks in my heart. What are the sparks in our lives?

Sparks of hurt:

- Disappointments
- Rejection
- Lack of trust

Sparks of unforgiveness

- Been hurt
- Abused
- Let down

Sparks of Anger:

- Been lied to
- Been used

Sparks of guilt:

- Hiding something
- Secret sin
- Past experience

Sparks of bitterness:

- Refuse to give another chance

THE BIGGER THE FIRE, THE MORE THE SPARKS

The sparks fly away and dissipate, the hotter the fire the more sparks. So, get "on fire" and watch them fly.

1. Read the Word of God
2. Be faithful to the House of God
3. Be obedient to His Word
4. Daily devotional
5. Serve others
6. Get involved in your local church

You may ask, how can you do this? Get intimate with God.

1. Rest in His presence
2. Become transparent
3. Listen to His *still small voice*

February 25

TARRY

And being assembled together with them, He commanded them not to depart from Jerusalem, but to wait for the Promise of the Father, "which," He said, "you have heard from Me; for John truly baptized with water, but you shall be baptized with the Holy Spirit not many days from now."(Acts 1:4-5)(NKJV)

Tarry means to surrender…your time, feelings and will. You cannot get intimate with someone you do not spend time with. When we get intimate with God, He becomes the lover of our soul and fills us with passion for Him.

No matter what you are facing…**make time** to be with God.

When was the last time you heard His *still small voice?*

February 26

WHY GO BACK TO SLAVERY?

When the LORD began to speak by Hosea, the LORD said to Hosea:
"Go, take yourself a wife of harlotry and children of harlotry,
For the land has committed great harlotry
by departing from the LORD." (Hosea 1:2)(NKJV)

The Lord told Hosea to marry a prostitute and they had two sons and one daughter together. God used Hosea's life/marriage as a prophetic example to Israel because they were enjoying a temporary period of economic prosperity and political peace that produced a false sense of security. They did not think they had any need for God because their needs were met in their own way.

After years of love and devotion by Hosea, his wife Gomer left to go back into the world. She had a husband who accepted her the way she was, loved, protected and provided for her and yet went back into slavery. The Bible says in Ch.2:6-7 she had no peace, (a false sense of security?) As far as Hosea...can you believe it? He bought her back. Are you enslaved, stuck in a rut, in quick-sand and being sucked under? Are you wrestling with something and can't seem to get victory over it?

Gomer sinned like Israel sinned. She walked away from the one who loved her, provided and protected her...she was sorry...and Hosea took her back. (ONLY GOD'S LOVE) Gomer, like Israel sinned...Hosea took her back (and loved her). Have you sinned? God wants you back! He will NEVER leave you or forsake you. Cry out to Him...Wait.... listen…. for His… *still small voice.*

February 27

PASSION TO HEAR GOD'S VOICE

The voice of the LORD is over the waters; The God of glory thunders;
The LORD is over many waters. The voice of the LORD is powerful;
The voice of the LORD is full of majesty. The voice of the LORD
breaks the cedars, Yes, the LORD splinters the cedars of Lebanon.
He makes them also skip like a calf, Lebanon and Sirion like a
young wild ox. The voice of the LORD divides the flames of fire.
The voice of the LORD shakes the wilderness; The LORD shakes
the Wilderness of Kadesh. The voice of the LORD makes
the deer give birth, And strips the forests bare; And in His
temple everyone says, "Glory!" (Psalm 29:3-9)(NKJV)

Who can create the thunders? God speaks and something happens. Think about your eyelashes, toenails, teeth. Did you ever think why your teeth don't keep growing or how your toenails keep replenishing themselves? Because God's voice commanded your body to grow and His voice is precise and powerful.

A cedar tree is humongous. At the base it has large tree like trunks that grow out from the main trunk. It's known for its strength and grows in Lebanon. God's voice can break the cedar tree!

What do we keep in our cedar chests? Valuables, woolens, furs, etc. - idols? Do you care too much about the things you have and protect them more than your relationship with the Lord? God's voice can break these things in our lives.

Lord, I don't want anything in my life that will take my attention away from you, much less be an idol. You are the only one I want to worship. Speak to me...Let me hear your *still small voice*.

February 28

PASSION TO BE LIKE JESUS

Then Jesus went about all the cities and villages, teaching in their synagogues, preaching the gospel of the kingdom, and healing every sickness and every disease among the people. But when He saw the multitudes, He was moved with compassion for them, because they were weary and scattered, like sheep having no shepherd. Then He said to His disciples, "The harvest truly is plentiful, but the laborers are few. Therefore pray the Lord of the harvest to send out laborers into His harvest." (Matthew 9:35-38)(NKJV)

The Lord wants us to have compassion on others...everybody; to teach, preach, heal, have compassion - to have compassion on the sick and the lost, to have authority over the enemy and anger towards sin. It will not always be easy but if we want to be like Jesus we must have the compassion of Jesus. John the Baptist was beheaded for Christ.

- When we are willing to lose our own life...that is passion.
- Remember...Jesus had a passion for you

To be like Jesus we need:

- A passion for His Word
- A passion for His Voice
- A passion for His Will
- A passion for Him!

OH, TO BE LIKE JESUS

February 29

HIS PRESENCE – HIS TOUCH

Then Jesus entered and passed through Jericho. Now behold, there was a man named Zacchaeus who was a chief tax collector, and he was rich. And he sought to see who Jesus was, but could not because of the crowd, for he was of short stature. So, he ran ahead and climbed up into a sycamore tree to see Him, for He was going to pass that way. And when Jesus came to the place, He looked up and saw him, and said to him, "Zacchaeus, make haste and come down, for today I must stay at your house." So, he made haste and came down, and received Him joyfully. But when they saw it, they all complained, saying, "He has gone to be a guest with a man who is a sinner." Then Zacchaeus stood and said to the Lord, "Look, Lord, I give half of my goods to the poor; and if I have taken anything from anyone by false accusation, I restore fourfold." And Jesus said to him, "Today salvation has come to this house, because he also is a son of Abraham; for the Son of Man has come to seek and to save that which was lost." (Luke 19:1-10)(NKJV)

Zacchaeus was a chief tax collector and had collected more than he should, which made him a much-disliked man. Knowing Jesus was passing through Jericho his curiosity was looking forward to seeing Him. Being such a small man in stature the only way he knew for sure to see Jesus through the crowd was to climb up into a tree. (Zacchaeus was determined...he was passionate about seeing Jesus) Salvation came to Zacchaeus' house that day!

Jesus was not looking for perfection only a heart with a passion for Him. People did not like Zacchaeus, but Jesus did. In all his dishonesty Jesus accepted him, because He knew that once salvation came to Zacchaeus' life, he would be changed.

- Don't let your feelings keep you from God's presence, He accepted Zacchaeus and He'll accept you.
- Just the <u>presence</u> of Jesus changed Zacchaeus' heart

Zacchaeus made a great effort for the presence of Jesus…make the effort and His presence, His touch will change your life forever. This is a "New Day" and I will continue to "rejoice" in it!
You are my God, you are my guide. Please let this day bring glory and honor to you Father, In Jesus name.

★ ★ ★

6:45 AM
It's a blue glow as the daylight peeks through the sky with a touch of frost dusting the earth with lingering snow caps as if the Master Himself strategically placed them in their rightful spots. (Oh, He did!) Through the frost and glow of a new day dawning rustic leaves are nestled within the rocks. How beautiful it is here in the Poconos. God bless Joe and Sue, this cabin is so warm and cozy, yet graced with a touch of elegance. (Sue—that's the woman's touch)

March 1

MIRACLE ON 94ᵀᴴ STREET
(PART ONE)

While He spoke these things to them, behold, a ruler came and worshiped
Him, saying, "My daughter has just died, but come and lay Your hand
on her and she will live." So Jesus arose and followed him, and so did
His disciples. And suddenly, a woman who had a flow of blood for twelve
years came from behind and touched the hem of His garment. For she said
to herself, "If only I may touch His garment, I shall be made well." But
Jesus turned around, and when He saw her He said, "Be of good cheer,
daughter; your faith has made you well." And the woman was made
well from that hour. When Jesus came into the ruler's house, and saw
the flute players and the noisy crowd wailing, He said to them, "Make
room, for the girl is not dead, but sleeping." And they ridiculed Him. But
when the crowd was put outside, He went in and took her by the hand,
and the girl arose. And the report of this went out into all that land.
(Matthew 9:18-26)(NKJV)

When my family and I moved back home to NJ from living in MO for
seven years, we did not want to just jump into buying a house so we prayed
to see where God wanted us to be. On 3/24/02 the Lord directed me to
II Sam. 7:10-11(KJV)

Moreover, I will appoint a place for my people Israel, and will plant
them, that they may dwell in a place of their own, and move no more;
neither shall the children of wickedness afflict them any more, as
beforetime, And as since the time that I commanded judges to be over
my people Israel, and have caused thee to rest from all thine enemies.
Also the LORD telleth thee that He will make thee a house.
(II Sam. 7:10-11)(KJV)

Months later while fasting and praying my husband barged into the house with tears rolling down his face. The Lord had given him a similar scripture along with a direct spot on the map of NJ. Our search began...We finally found the one...eleven months

March 2

MIRACLE ON 94TH STREET (PART TWO)

later and still no closing. Everything that could go wrong did. But we held onto God's Word!

- Hold on to His Word
- He is faithful!
- Watch what happens

You see in this scripture the woman was ill for many years but still believed. The little girl was dead but…Jesus came on the scene, when Jesus comes on the scene SOMETHING IS GOING TO HAPPEN! They mocked Jesus because he said the girl was not dead just sleeping. Wow! You see Jesus sees things differently than we do. His ways and thoughts are not like ours. As you can see the woman was healed and the little girl lived!

12/29/03 Hallelujah the day of the closing! Judges 18:9-10 (KJV) is what the Lord blessed us with that day:

> *And they said, Arise, that we may go up against them: for we have*
> *seen the land, and, behold, it is very good: and are ye still?*
> *Be not slothful to go, and to enter to possess the land.*
> *When ye go, ye shall come unto a people secure, and to a large land:*
> *for God hath given it into your hands; a place where there is no*
> *want of anything that is in the earth. (Judges 18:9-10) (KJV)*

The house is on 94th Street.

Even though it looks like it's dead…who said it was?

March 3

GET UP ON THE HILL

And Moses said to Joshua, "Choose us some men and go out, fight with Amalek. Tomorrow I will stand on the top of the hill with the rod of God in my hand." (Exodus 17:9)(NKJV)

And Moses went up to God, and the Lord called to him from the mountain, saying, "Thus you shall say to the house of Jacob, and tell the children of Israel" (Exodus 19:3)(NKJV)

Then the Lord came down upon Mount Sinai, on the top of the mountain. And the Lord called Moses to the top of the mountain, and Moses went up. (Exodus 19:20)(NKJV)

Many times in war, the leader will go to the top and look down as it's better to see what the enemy is doing.

- You've got to get to the mountain top in order to see what's going on.

It's not always easy climbing to the top with rocks and branches to trip you up. It's not easy going against gravity; it is easy to get hurt. But it is necessary! There are branches of fear, rocks of hurt - you can fall over them and get hurt or you can step on them to get closer to the top.

Your word is a lamp to my feet
And a light to my path. (Ps. 119:105)(NKJV)

- You can do it!
- Let God's Word guide you

March 4

THE CHALLENGE

"Repent, for the kingdom of heaven is at hand!"
(Matthew 3:2)(NKJV)

Make that free will decision to STOP doing anything contrary to the Word of God. Repentance is made possible by the enabling grace that's given to you as you hear and believe the Gospel of Jesus Christ.

Therefore I say to you, her sins, which are many, are
forgiven, for she loved much. But to whom little is
forgiven, the same loves little." (Luke 7:47)(NKJV)

This woman washed Jesus feet with her tears…would you?

* He forgives you because He loves you

So when they had eaten breakfast, Jesus said to Simon Peter,
"Simon, son of Jonah, do you love Me more than these?"
He said to Him, "Yes, Lord; You know that I love You."
He said to him, "Feed My lambs."(John 21:15)(NKJV)

* Listen to that *still small voice*

★ ★ ★

I think it is becoming a blizzard out there. Snow covered ground with tall grey stalk like trees stretched toward heaven. Wood crackling in the fire… can you hear it? The stillness is indescribable.

March 5

ACQUAINTED WITH GRIEF

He is despised and rejected by men,
A Man of sorrows and acquainted with grief.
And we hid, as it were, our faces from Him;
He was despised, and we did not esteem Him.
Surely He has borne our griefs
And carried our sorrows;
Yet we esteemed Him stricken,
Smitten by God, and afflicted.
But He was wounded for our transgressions,
He was bruised for our iniquities;
The chastisement for our peace was upon Him,
And by His stripes we are healed.
All we like sheep have gone astray;
We have turned, every one, to his own way;
And the Lord has laid on Him the iniquity of us all.
(Isaiah 53:3-6)(NKJV)

He was neither attractive nor popular, He was rejected and a man of sorrows. He carried a heavy load.

- He took your punishment
- He took your place
- Your peace comes from Him
- Your healing comes from Him

After all He's done…how can you not trust Him?

March 6

WATCH!

"Watch therefore, for you know neither the day nor the hour in which the Son of Man is coming." (Matthew 25:13)(NKJV)

This verse in the Amplified Version says: "Give strict attention and be cautious" and in The New American Standard Version it says: "Be on the alert".

This chapter is discussing the five foolish and five wise virgins. Five virgins were ready for their bridegroom but five were not. It's easy to say: "oh I have time" or "it will never happen to me" The wise virgins were prepared.

- Don't be asleep
- Prepare yourself for His coming
- Be ready

March 7

FACE TO FACE

But since then there has not arisen in Israel a prophet like Moses, whom the LORD knew face to face, in all the signs and wonders which the LORD sent him to do in the land of Egypt, before Pharaoh, before all his servants, and in all his land, (Deuteronomy 34:10-11)(NKJV)

Scripture says that the Lord knew Moses face to face. Do you realize that was through the plagues in Egypt? There was Blood, frogs, lice, flies, death of all cattle, boils, hail, locusts, total darkness, and the death of the Egyptians' first born. Whew...I'm glad I wasn't an Egyptian!

You see the Lord knew that Moses would trust Him because in Exodus God told Moses that He would be with him. As always...God kept His Word!

Just because you go through things in this life, some more unbearable than others, it does not mean that God does not know where or who you are. He knows EXACTLY where and who you are.

It's when we go through something that we see God, face to face.

★ ★ ★

I believe there must be an inch of snow out there. Since I'm "stuck" here I thought I'd pop some chocolate chip cookies into the oven...can you smell them? Oooooh snow falling, wood crackling, the smell of chocolate chip cookies, God is so good! If I can't hear God's *small still voice* in this environment...I must be dead.

March 8

BEYOND FAITH

Nebuchadnezzar spoke, saying to them, "Is it true, Shadrach,
Meshach, and Abednego, that you do not serve my gods or worship
the gold image which I have set up? Now if you are ready at the time
you hear the sound of the horn, flute, harp, lyre, and psaltery, in
symphony with all kinds of music, and you fall down and worship
the image which I have made, good! But if you do not worship, you
shall be cast immediately into the midst of a burning fiery furnace.
And who is the god who will deliver you from my hands?"
Shadrach, Meshach, and Abednego answered and said to the king,
"O Nebuchadnezzar, we have no need to answer you in this matter.
If that is the case, our God whom we serve is able to deliver us from
the burning fiery furnace, and He will deliver us from your hand, O
king. But if not, let it be known to you, O king, that we do not serve
your gods, nor will we worship the gold image which you have set
up." Then Nebuchadnezzar was full of fury, and the expression on
his face changed toward Shadrach, Meshach, and Abednego. He spoke
and commanded that they heat the furnace seven times more than it
was usually heated. And he commanded certain mighty men of valor
who were in his army to bind Shadrach, Meshach, and Abednego, and
cast them into the burning fiery furnace. Then these men were bound
in their coats, their trousers, their turbans, and their other garments,
and were cast into the midst of the burning fiery furnace. Therefore,
because the king's command was urgent, and the furnace exceedingly
hot, the flame of the fire killed those men who took up Shadrach,
Meshach, and Abednego. And these three men, Shadrach, Meshach, and
Abednego, fell down bound into the midst of the burning fiery furnace.
Then King Nebuchadnezzar was astonished; and he rose in haste
and spoke, saying to his counselors, "Did we not cast three men

bound into the midst of the fire?" They answered and said to the king, "True, O king." "Look!" he answered, "I see four men loose, walking in the midst of the fire; and they are not hurt, and the form of the fourth is like the Son of God."(Daniel 3:14–25)(NKJV)

March 9

THE ENEMY IS NERVOUS!

Daniel chapter 3…read it

No matter how hot the furnace was when King Nebuchadnezzar was to throw Shadrach, Meshach and Abednego in, it was still hot enough. It was hot enough to kill anyone. However, the reason for him ordering that the furnace be turned up seven times hotter was because he was getting nervous. These three young men had such a steadfast faith in their God that it shook the king. Their faith was causing the king to cower. You see even though his actions were strong, it was in desperation as he could not kill their faith.

When you and I stand strong on God's Word and hold on, we make the enemy nervous. He then knows he is defeated. So…when the heat is turned up in your life…know that the enemy is nervous!

Hallelujah…you may be in the furnace but look around…you're not alone!

March 10

HOW BIG IS YOUR GOD?

So she said, "As the LORD your God lives, I do not have bread, only a handful of flour in a bin, and a little oil in a jar; and see, I am gathering a couple of sticks that I may go in and prepare it for myself and my son, that we may eat it, and die." And Elijah said to her, "Do not fear; go and do as you have said, but make me a small cake from it first, and bring it to me; and afterward make some for yourself and your son. For thus says the LORD God of Israel: 'The bin of flour shall not be used up, nor shall the jar of oil run dry, until the day the LORD sends rain on the earth.'" So she went away and did according to the word of Elijah; and she and he and her household ate for many days. The bin of flour was not used up, nor did the jar of oil run dry, according to the word of the LORD which He spoke by Elijah (I Kings 17:12-16)(NKJV)

This woman had only enough food to make one last meal for her and her son before they would starve to death…so she thought. The man of God came along and said feed me first. What!? Well, she trusted his words because he said; The Lord said her oil and flour would never run out. She obeyed in faith and God was true to His Word.

The song says:

> He walks with me and
> He talks with me, and
> He tells me I am His own,

And the joy we share
As we tarry there
None other has ever known.[7]

HOW BIG IS YOUR GOD?

★　★　★

Would you believe someone just rode by on a lime green snowmobile? The snow is hard and heavy, the stove is cranking and the cookies were yummy. It's cold outside but it's warm and toasty in here. God is so good!

---

[7] *In The Garden,* Words and Music by C. Austin Miles, 1912, Public Domain.

March 11

AN OFFERING IN RIGHTOUSNESS

Read the book of Malachi, it only has four small chapters

When the book of Malachi is mentioned, immediately the subject of tithing comes to mind, however that is not so. God was burdened for Israel because of His love for them. He was not happy with their lifestyle and wanted to let them know. They did not honor God's name and offered second hand offerings to Him. You see the Lord does not want your money, He wants you. The command to tithe is correct, but if we want to be blessed you must give more than your money. You must give Him your all. In the book of Malachi, He was basically saying that they needed to "BE" an offering in righteousness, then you tithe because you WANT to not because you have to.

- God wants our best
- Think of all He's done for you

Results of obedience:

- He will open up heaven and pour out blessings that you wouldn't have room enough to contain them (Ch.3:10)
- He will rebuke the devourer (Ch. 3:11) that's not just in finances, it's in all areas the enemy is trying to rob.
- He will reunite the family (Ch.4:6)

He doesn't want your sacrifice, He wants you.

- It's time to spend some quiet time and LISTEN to His *still small voice*

March 12

POWER IN WAITING

Have you not known?
Have you not heard?
The everlasting God, the LORD,
The Creator of the ends of the earth,
Neither faints nor is weary.
His understanding is unsearchable.
He gives power to the weak,
And to those who have no might He increases strength.
Even the youths shall faint and be weary,
And the young men shall utterly fall,
But those who wait on the LORD
Shall renew their strength;
They shall mount up with wings like eagles,
They shall run and not be weary,
They shall walk and not faint. (Isaiah 40:28-31)(NKJV)

God cared about His people Israel during a time of political and national decline. He saw their battle with the Assyrian Army and just wanted to let them know that their strength will come from Him.

Wait - 1. To <u>stay in one place</u>, to <u>anticipate</u> or <u>expect</u> something.

      2. To <u>stay</u>, <u>rest</u>, to <u>remain stationary</u> in <u>expectation</u> of.

- Haven't you tried in your own strength long enough?
- Wait on the Lord
- Listen to His *still small voice*

March 13

DON'T LOOK DOWN!

Now in the fourth watch of the night Jesus went to them, walking on the sea.
And when the disciples saw Him walking on the sea, they were troubled,
saying, "It is a ghost!" And they cried out for fear. But immediately Jesus
spoke to them, saying, "Be of good cheer! It is I; do not be afraid." And
Peter answered Him and said, "Lord, if it is You, command me to come
to You on the water." So He said, "Come." And when Peter had come
down out of the boat, he walked on the water to go to Jesus. But when he
saw that the wind was boisterous, he was afraid; and beginning to sink
he cried out, saying, "Lord, save me!" And immediately Jesus stretched
out His hand and caught him, and said to him, "O you of little faith,
why did you doubt? And when they got into the boat, the wind ceased.
(Matthew 14:25-32)(NKJV)

After multiplying the fish and loaves of bread to feed more than five
thousand the disciples were now in their boat. A storm was raging, first
they were rejoicing in the miracle and now a storm. They were afraid;
they saw a figure on the water and did not recognize it being Jesus. Peter
asked Jesus to let him walk on the water as well. As long as Peter kept his
eyes on Jesus he actually did walk on the water but as soon as the storm got
progressed he began to be fearful and sink. Jesus caught him.

We go through storms and even though we too have experienced the Hand
of God at times we still find ourselves fearful. Our eyes are looking at the
surroundings, not on the one who can make us walk on water. Jesus was
still faithful to catch Peter and he'll catch you too.

- Don't be amazed when you're living in the strength of God
- Keep your eyes on Jesus

March 14

WHO IS GOD?

"God is not a man, that He should lie,
Nor a son of man, that He should repent.
Has He said, and will He not do?
Or has He spoken, and will He not make it good?
(Numbers 23:19)(NKJV)

How many times has The Lord spoken to you and lied?

NEVER!!!!! CAN'T HAPPEN!!!

So…No matter how long you are waiting for your answer to come, do not give up because:

- God is a man of honor
- He is not a man who lies
- He is faithful
- If He said it, it will be

March 15

WHERE DID GOD COME FROM?

In the beginning God created the heavens and the earth.
(Genesis 1:1)(NKJV)

"In the beginning" that tells me that God "always was". I know that seems hard to understand, but do you understand everything anyway? Do you know how your car works or what makes your electricity go on? Do you know how the stars suspend in air or why it snows in the winter and not in the summer? Oh yes, because it's too hot...who made the seasons? Bottom line is we will never understand everything. We must accept the Word of God as "final"

- In the beginning tells me, God always was!
- Walk by faith

March 16

WHAT IS GOD?

*Then God said, "Let there be light"; and there was light
(Genesis 1:3)(NKJV)*

*Then God said, "Let there be a firmament in the midst of the waters,
and let it divide the waters from the waters." (Genesis 1:6)(NJKV)*

*Then God said, "Let the waters under the heavens be
gathered together into one place, and let the dry land
appear"; and it was so. (Genesis 1:9)(NKJV)*

*Then God said, "Let the earth bring forth grass, the herb that yields
seed, and the fruit tree that yields fruit according to its kind, whose
seed is in itself, on the earth"; and it was so. (Genesis 1:11)(NKJV)*

*Then God said, "Let there be lights in the firmament of the
heavens to divide the day from the night; and let them be for signs
and seasons, and for days and years ;(Genesis 1:14)(NKJV)*

*Then God said, "Let the waters abound with an abundance of
living creatures, and let birds fly above the earth across the face
of the firmament of the heavens." (Genesis 1:20)(NKJV)*

*Then God said, "Let the earth bring forth the living creature
according to its kind: cattle and creeping things and beasts of
the earth, each according to its kind"; and it was so.
(Genesis 1:24)(NKJV)*

- Creator of light and darkness
- Creator of day and night
- Creator of plants and animals
- He is the giver of life *(Gen.1:26-28)*
- He's all powerful *(Matt. 28:18)*
- In Exodus He is a warrior and way maker
- In John He's the Word, our Savior, comforter and provider

What isn't He?

March 17

GOD:

(From Genesis to Revelation)

- WILL NOT LIE!
- ALWAYS WAS
- IS YOUR CREATOR
- IS YOUR GIVER OF LIFE
- IS ALL POWERFUL
- IS YOUR DELIVERER
- IS YOUR WARRIOR
- IS THE WORD
- YOUR SAVIOR
- LOVES YOU
- HAS MERCY ON YOU
- MADE YOUR WAY TO HEAVEN
- IS YOUR COMFORTER
- IS YOUR PROVIDER
- GOD IS...

March 18

IF YOU ONLY KNEW!

Jesus answered and said to her, "If you knew the gift of God, and who it is who says to you, 'Give Me a drink,' you would have asked Him, and He would have given you living water."
(John 4:10)(NKJV)

Jesus being thirsty from His journey asked this woman at the well for a drink of water. Oh, but the Jews had no dealing with Samaritans. Knowing this, the woman is taken back by his request for a drink. Jesus makes it very clear to her that He was not just some ordinary man but He was the "living water", that if she would partake in Him she would "never thirst again"

Jesus isn't looking at your nationality, financial status or background, He's looking at you. He loves YOU! If you only knew how much He loves you, you too would be shouting like the woman at the well.

March 19

PERFECT-PERFECTION-PERFECTED

"You have heard that it was said, 'You shall love your neighbor and hate your enemy.' But I say to you, love your enemies, bless those who curse you, do good to those who hate you, and pray for those who spitefully use you and persecute you, that you may be sons of your Father in heaven; for He makes His sun rise on the evil and on the good, and sends rain on the just and on the unjust. For if you love those who love you, what reward have you? Do not even the tax collectors do the same? And if you greet your brethren only, what do you do more than others? Do not even the tax collectors do so? Therefore you shall be perfect, just as your Father in heaven is perfect. (Matthew 5:43-48)(NKJV)

There will only ever be one perfect one and His name is Jesus. Why should we look for perfection in someone else when we are not?

Perfect: Complete in all respects; without defect; sound; flawless, faultless, completely correct.

Are you:

- Complete in all respects?
- Without defects?
- Flawless?
- Faultless?
- Completely correct?

Only Jesus is perfect, we are all in the process of perfection and will never be perfected until we are in heaven.

- Are you dead? If not...Ask God to help you with that one that is like sand paper.
- Listen to His *still small voice*

March 20

HAPPY BIRTHDAY GIDEON

Gideon
Meaning: Great Warrior

My Gideon Isaac, that smile, those eyes; Gideon, you with your blond hair
and blue eyes melt my heart. I get pure joy watching the things you do as
there are so many traits similar to your daddy and it makes me remember
him as a little boy. Your love for guns, guns, and more guns; every time I
ask what I could get you, it's the same answer...a gun. If you don't have a
gun in your hand it's a tool. You are always fixing something, again like
your daddy. I think even as a toddler you would love to own your own
motorcycle. My beautiful, adorable little Gideon; how I love you. I see
how you tease Mia, you sneaky Pete. (smile) I see the little things you do
thinking no one is watching (just like your dad did at your age) and that
sly little stare with just a bit of a smirk and I love you for it. I love to hear
you talk like only you can. Cuddling with you and reading a story when
you rush me to get to the end...I love you so much! You are a gift from
God to Grandpa and I and we will cherish you always.

Gideon, I believe one day you will be as your name states: a great warrior
only for God. I can see you determined to win no matter how you have to
do it. You're a good boy Gideon, I pray that you would always love Jesus
with all your heart, soul, mind and strength. I pray that He will keep you
safe and strong and that you will want for nothing, ever, all the days of
your life. I pray blessings upon you and with an expectancy to see them
come to pass. Mighty little warrior...HAPPY BIRTHDAY Gideon Isaac,
I love you so much!!! Nonna

March 21

DEAD MEN DON'T CARE!

What shall we say then? Shall we continue in sin, that grace may abound? God forbid. How shall we, that are dead to sin, live any longer therein? Know ye not, that so many of us as were baptized into Jesus Christ were baptized into his death? Therefore we are buried with him by baptism into death: that like as Christ was raised up from the dead by the glory of the Father, even so we also should walk in newness of life. (Romans 6:1-4) (KJV)

Did you ever see a dead man yell, or flirt, or complain? Of course, you haven't because a dead man is dead. There is not life in him to speak or have feelings in any way. If you are dead in Christ then the old man is gone, there is no life to the old man. You will not be offended because you're dead, you won't be tempted because you're dead. You can't have your own way because you're dead.

If the old man is coming back to life tell him to "drop dead!"

- Find a place to be alone with the Lord

We all have our struggles, you are no different but…we've got to let it die.

- Listen to your new life giver's *still small voice*

March 22

WHAT IS THAT IN YOUR HAND?

*At Joppa there was a certain disciple named Tabitha, which
is translated Dorcas. This woman was full of good works
and charitable deeds which she did. (Acts 9:36)(NKJV)*

Dorcas was a follower of Jesus and out of the love in her heart she wanted
to help people. She was a seamstress who sewed coats for those who did
not have the means to purchase one on their own. She cared! When Dorcas
died the mourners called Peter to show him all the garments she made for
them. Let me ask you…what can you do for the Lord? Do you have to
get paid?

Let me tell you about Jerry; Jerry is a gentleman in my home church who
has a bit of a disability…. but not in God's eyes. Jerry is our "head usher"
he also makes a phone call to every single member of the church every
single Saturday Night reminding them to be in Sunday Morning Service.
For more than twenty years Jerry has never missed calling my home
reminding my family to be in church. Jerry is a "HUGE" success. What
is it that you can do?

Dorcas:

- Was not selfish
- Was not self-seeking
- Did not have to be seen
- Left behind a legacy

Dorcas had some purple thread; Jerry has a telephone, what's in your hand?

March 23

JESUS USE ME

There's a song that goes like this:

Jesus, use me
And oh Lord, don't refuse me
For surely there's a work
That I can do
And even though it's humble
Lord help my will to crumble
Though the cost be great
I'll work for you[8]

Not my will Lord, but yours

Let Him speak to you through His ***still small voice***

March 24

I CAN ONLY IMAGINE

The words to another song:

> I can only imagine what it will be like, when I walk, by your side
> I can only imagine what my eyes will see, When you face
> is before me. I can only imagine, I can only imagine
>
> Surrounded by your glory, what will my heart feel?
> Will I dance for you Jesus, or in awe of you be still
> Will I stand in your presence, or to my knees will I fall
> Will I sing hallelujah, Will I be able to speak at all?
> I can only imagine.[9]

Did you realize that He's here with you right now?

March 25

HOW DO I HANDLE DISAPPOINTMENTS?

*Be anxious for nothing, but in everything by prayer and
supplication, with thanksgiving, let your requests be made known
to God; and the peace of God, which surpasses all understanding,
will guard your hearts and minds through Christ Jesus.
Finally, brethren, whatever things are true, whatever things
are noble, whatever things are just, whatever things are pure,
whatever things are lovely, whatever things are of good report,
if there is any virtue and if there is anything praiseworthy—
meditate on these things (Philippians 4:6-8)(NKJV)*

- How does this affect my salvation?
- Pray
- Have a heart of thanksgiving
- Keep your nose in "The Book"

March 26

HOW HARD IS IT?

I can do all things through Christ who strengthens me.
(Philippians 4:13)(NKJV)

We all struggle, some more than others, but what do we do with the struggle? Do we quit? Give up? Has it been hard? Maybe it's been a long time and no matter what you do it doesn't change.... don't give in to the voices of defeat. Know that if you try on your own you may fail but if you surrender to Jesus...let Him know you want victory but it's a struggle. He knows already but He may be waiting for you to surrender it and trust Him. Remember:

YOU CAN do ALL things THROUGH CHRIST WHO STRENGTHENS YOU.

March 27

TRUTH – FREEDOM

The grass withers, the flower fades,
But the Word of our God stands forever." (Isaiah 40:8)(NKJV)

Josiah became king in Judah at eight years old, the Lord told him to rebuild the House of God. At age sixteen not knowing where to start first he began to seek God. (Best thing to do) Josiah was not raised to fear God. While repairing the House of God the "book of the law" was found. The Word of God began to humble him of wrong doings. The Word began to cleanse, guide and teach him how to set Judah free. Manasseh who was Josiah's grandfather thought he had destroyed all the Word of God but the scripture lives on.

You may not know what to do next, maybe you're like Josiah feeling too young to know what to do next. Is this binding you, you just don't feel free?

Get into the Word and you'll know the truth

March 28

WE'RE CREATING MEMORIES HERE

And we know that all things work together for good to those who
love God, to those who are the called according to His purpose.
(Romans 8:28)(NKJV)

While waiting for the closing on our home in NJ we lived in a travel trailer. The only phone we had was a cellular phone. We quickly found out that being in a wooded campground made it impossible for us to get a connection. We did however discover that there was a ceramic watermelon on the ledge behind the sofa and if we put our head into it we could hear and the other party could hear us as well. Needless to say, if one of us called a family member from outside the trailer we would shout;

"PUT YOUR HEAD IN THE WATERMELON!" This was outrageous! Not realizing it, we would shout that wherever we were, (even in public places) do you think people thought we were a quart low? Of course! But you see it wasn't forever.

Everything we do in life is creating memories. Not all memories are good ones but they are memories still the same. Look at it this way; if you love Jesus, this is just a test and if you TRULY love Jesus this test will become a testimony.

- So, smile, memories are being created.
- "PUT YOUR HEAD IN THE WATERMELON!"

March 29

NOT MY WILL LORD

Then they came to a place which was named Gethsemane; and
He said to His disciples, "Sit here while I pray." And He took
Peter, James, and John with Him, and He began to be troubled
and deeply distressed. ³⁴Then He said to them, "My soul is
exceedingly sorrowful, even to death. Stay here and watch."
He went a little farther, and fell on the ground, and prayed that
if it were possible, the hour might pass from Him. And He said,
"Abba, Father, all things are possible for You. Take this cup away
from Me; nevertheless, not what I will, but what You will."
Then He came and found them sleeping, and said to Peter, "Simon, are
you sleeping? Could you not watch one hour? (Mark 14:32-37)(NKJV)

Jesus began to feel the emotional pain, agony of what was to come. Her fell to the ground and cried out to God. Jesus had a passion (compelling urgency) to be in the Father's presence as He knew what was ahead. His desire was to do the Father's Will.

Listen:

- It's not all about me
- It's not where I want to go
- It's not what I want
- It's not what I want to do

What will come out of what "I" want? God's Will is not always going to be easy, but it wasn't easy for Jesus either and we are still reaping the benefits.

Salvation, freedom from sin, joy, peace and a sure way to heaven and the blessings go on and on and on...from generation to generation.

- His Will may not be easy but it will ALWAYS be rewarding
- What is His Will for your situation?
- Let Him speak to you through His *still small voice*

March 30

ONE LANE BRIDGE

"Enter by the narrow gate; for wide is the gate and broad is the way that leads to destruction, and there are many who go in by it. Because narrow is the gate and difficult is the way which leads to life, and there are few who find it. (Matthew 7:13-14)(NKJV)

Until recently near my home was a one lane bridge. Before entering the bridge, the driver must look for the sign preparing you for the one lane bridge and proceed with caution. You never know if there could be an oncoming vehicle. This reminds me of this verse in scripture.

Sometimes we get stressed out over circumstances, but our main focus should be on making it to heaven. If my mind was not on the signs or the upcoming (one lane) bridge I could be in an accident. I must not be distracted!

Don't let anything cause you to lose your attention; keep your focus on heaven.

Never mind anyone else, just make sure you're clear to go.

March 31

UP ON THE ROOF

"Come now, and let us reason together,"
Says the LORD,
"Though your sins are like scarlet,
They shall be as white as snow;
Though they are red like crimson,
They shall be as wool (Isaiah 1:18)(NKJV)

There's a song called *Up On The Roof* from the 1960s that I'm sure we can all relate to. Many days we just want to get away (especially if we want to hide something). This Word of hope says that we should talk to the Lord… no matter what, He can make it right.

You don't need a roof when you have a Heavenly Father.